Bryn Mawr Latin Commentaries

Editors

Julia Haig Gaisser   James J. O'Donnell

Bryn Mawr College   *University of Pennsylvania*

The purpose of the Bryn Mawr Latin Commentaries is to make a wide range of classical and post-classical authors accessible to the intermediate student. Each commentary provides the minimum grammatical and lexical information necessary for a first reading of the text.

Bryn Mawr Latin Commentaries

Nepos
Life of Atticus

Cynthia Damon

Thomas Library
Bryn Mawr College

The Bryn Mawr Latin Commentaries are supported by a generous grant from the Division of Education Programs of the National Endowment for the Humanities

Copyright ©1993 by Bryn Mawr College

Manufactured in the United States of America

ISBN-0-929524-81-0

Printed and distributed by:
Bryn Mawr Commentaries
Thomas Library
Bryn Mawr College
101 North Merion Avenue
Bryn Mawr, PA 19010

INTRODUCTION

Cornelius Nepos was a prolific encyclopedist writing in the last decades of the Roman Republic and in the first of Augustus' "restored" republic. Among other things he produced a universal history, the *Chronica* ("Times") and a large collection of brief biographies of noteworthy men from Greece, Rome and beyond (*de Viris Illustribus*). The first work earned him his most impressive testimonial: he is the Cornelius to whom Catullus dedicated his *libellus* (*ausus es unus Italorum/ omne aeuum tribus explicare cartis/ doctis, Iuppiter, et laboriosis*, c. 1.6-7).

We know too little about Nepos' life. He had made his way to Rome from his hometown in northern Italy by 65 BC, in time to hear Cicero's speech on behalf of the tribune Cornelius, but like his compatriot Catullus he seems to have played no active part in Roman politics. All that can be gleaned about his political sympathies is a certain hostility to the party of the "liberators" Brutus and Cassius (see 8.3-5 and 9.7 in the *Life of Atticus*) and an attraction to M. Antonius which lingered even after Antony's defeat (in 31 BC) and suicide (in 30). Nepos refused to go along with those who would have liked to consign Antony to ignominy or, better, oblivion (see, e.g., 10.4, 12.2). Both of these opinions stood in the way of a warm relationship with Cicero, and when Atticus recommends Nepos to Cicero in 44 BC Cicero's response is less than gracious (*Letters to Atticus*, 16.5.5, cf. 16.14.4). Nor was politics the only area of disagreement between the two: Nepos thought very little of the philosophical investigations to which Cicero devoted so much time and paper in his last years, and Cicero knew it (Nepos fr. 39, and Cicero, *Letters to Atticus* 16.5.5). However, Nepos must somehow have succeeded in soothing Cicero's irritation, for there were two volumes of Cicero's letters to Nepos circulating in antiquity (they have not come down to us). Nepos speaks very warmly of the published collection of *Letters to Atticus* (16.3-4), and produced a biography of Cicero which extended to more than one volume. Nepos survived both of his friends, living on until at least 27 BC.

The *Life of Atticus* belongs to Nepos' collection of biographies of famous men. This work—now extant only in part—was dedicated to Atticus himself (c. 110-32 BC), and was therefore written before Atticus' death. The *Life* as we have it now was expanded at some time between 32 and 27 BC (see 19.1). The biographies in *de Viris Illustribus* were arranged by sub-headings (e.g., *de Excellentibus Ducibus*, "on outstanding military leaders"); the *Life of Atticus* comes from the collection *de Latinis Historicis* ("on historians writing in Latin," see §18). At 22 chapters it is considerably longer than the average for the work as a whole (insofar as that is fairly represented by the extant portions—these range in length from 3 to 13 chapters, with 4 chapters being the most frequent), and is enriched by Nepos' first-hand knowledge of and enthusiasm for his subject. It is far the best of the extant collection.

To characterize the *Life* one needs to consider both what is present and what is not. It is organized around the moralizing text *sui cuique mores fingunt fortunam hominibus* "a man's character fashions his fate" (11.6, cf. 19.1), and little nuggets of moral instruction recur throughout (5.3, 10.6, 12.5, 15.1, 20.5

etc.). Chapters 13-17 even have moral qualities as rubrics: *comitas, humanitas, pietas*. But neither this ethical focus nor the exclusively laudatory angle adopted by Nepos prevents him from giving numerous precious historical details. He is particularly informative on the subject of Atticus' interaction with his (and Nepos') contemporaries (e.g., 5.3, 6.4, 7.3, 8.3, 9.4, etc.). Nepos also gives a fairly detailed survey of Atticus' literary output (§18). The nuances of Roman politics, however, are treated less well: the banality of the account of the Sullan period (the 80s BC, §§2-4) is perhaps understandable, but there is no discussion of the period 65-50 in which both Nepos and Atticus had a more direct experience of what was going on. The civil war between the Pompeians and Caesar (49-45) gets very short shrift (§7) and there is a disturbing inconcinnity between Cicero's account and that of Nepos here (see note on 7.3 *concesserit*). The *Life*, however, is full of valuable side-lights on the politics of the period just after Caesar's assassination in 44. Atticus' character, his friends and his writings, then, are the building blocks of this biography. What is left out? His family life, for one thing. Nepos twice refers to Atticus as a *pater familias* (4.4, 13.1), but in both places he means by this "property-owner" not "family man." In fact Atticus' slaves get more notice from Nepos than do his wife Pilia (whom he married in 56) and daughter Attica (who is mentioned only because she married a man with a great future—Agrippa—and produced a daughter with an even more distinguished husband—the emperor Tiberius). And even the coverage of Atticus as a property-owner is distinctly limited. Nepos tells us how Atticus spends his money (§13), but not how he makes it (apart from his two inheritances, of course). However partial (in both senses of the word) the biography is, it gives us unique information about a fascinating man who would otherwise be known to us only as the silent epistolary partner of a very voluble Cicero. Enigmatic he remains, but less so thanks to Nepos.

The text is my own, but it is heavily indebted to the works of P. K. Marshall listed in the Suggestions for Further Reading on p.14.

C.D.

Cambridge, Massachusetts
August 1993

EX LIBRO CORNELI NEPOTIS
DE LATINIS HISTORICIS

1 T. Pomponius Atticus, ab origine ultima stirpis Romanae generatus, perpetuo a maioribus acceptam equestrem obtinuit dignitatem. 2. patre usus est diligente et, ut tum erant tempora, diti inprimisque studioso litterarum. hic, prout ipse amabat litteras, omnibus doctrinis quibus puerilis aetas impertiri debet filium erudiuit. 3. erat autem in puero praeter docilitatem ingenii summa suauitas oris atque uocis, ut non solum celeriter acciperet quae tradebantur, sed etiam excellenter pronuntiaret. qua ex re in pueritia nobilis inter aequales ferebatur clariusque exsplendescebat quam <ut> generosi condiscipuli animo aequo ferre possent. 4. itaque incitabat omnes studio suo, quo in numero fuerunt L. Torquatus, C. Marius filius, M. Cicero. quos consuetudine sua sic deuinxit ut nemo iis perpetuo fuerit carior.

2 Pater mature decessit. ipse adulescentulus propter affinitatem P. Sulpici, qui tribunus pl. interfectus est, non expers fuit illius periculi. namque Anicia, Pomponi consobrina, nupserat Seruio, fratri Sulpici. 2. itaque interfecto Sulpicio posteaquam uidit Cinnano tumultu ciuitatem esse perturbatam neque sibi dari facultatem pro dignitate uiuendi quin alterutram partem offenderet, dissociatis animis ciuium, cum alii Sullanis, alii Cinnanis fauerent partibus, idoneum tempus ratus studiis obsequendi suis Athenas se contulit. neque eo setius adulescentem Marium hostem iudicatum iuuit opibus suis, cuius fugam pecunia subleuauit. 3. ac ne illa peregrinatio detrimentum aliquod afferret rei familiari, eodem magnam partem fortunarum traiecit suarum. hic ita uixit ut uniuersis Atheniensibus merito esset carissimus. 4. nam praeter gratiam, quae iam in adulescentulo magna erat, saepe suis opibus inopiam eorum publicam leuauit. cum enim uersuram facere publice necesse esset neque eius condicionem aequam haberent, semper se interposuit, atque ita ut neque usuram umquam ab iis acceperit neque longius quam dictum esset debere passus sit. 5. quod utrumque erat iis salutare: nam neque indulgendo inueterascere eorum aes alienum patiebatur neque multiplicandis usuris crescere. 6. auxit hoc officium alia quoque liberalitate: nam uniuersos frumento donauit, ita ut singulis seni modii tritici darentur, qui modus mensurae medimnus Athenis appellatur.

3 Hic autem sic se gerebat ut communis infimis, par principibus uideretur. quo factum est ut huic omnes honores, quos possent, publice haberent ciuemque facere studerent.[1] quo beneficio ille uti noluit. 2. quamdiu adfuit, ne qua sibi statua poneretur restitit; absens prohibere non potuit. itaque aliquot ipsi effigies[2] locis sanctissimis posuerunt. hunc enim in omni procuratione rei publicae actorem auctoremque habebant. 3. cui quidem[3] primum illud munus fortunae, quod in ea potissimum urbe natus est in qua domicilium orbis terrarum esset imperi, ut eandem et patriam haberet et domum, hoc specimen prudentiae, quod, cum in eam se ciuitatem contulisset quae antiquitate humanitate doctrinaque praestaret omnes, unus ei fuit carissimus.

4 Huc ex Asia Sulla decedens cum uenisset, quamdiu ibi fuit, secum habuit Pomponium, captus adulescentis et humanitate et doctrina. sic enim Graece loquebatur ut Athenis natus uideretur; tanta autem suauitas erat sermonis Latini ut appareret in eo natiuum quendam leporem esse, non ascitum. idem poemata pronuntiabat et Graece et Latine sic ut supra nihil posset addi. 2. quibus rebus factum est ut Sulla nusquam ab se dimitteret cuperetque secum deducere. qui cum persuadere tentaret, 'noli, oro te,' inquit Pomponius 'aduersum eos me uelle ducere, cum quibus ne contra te arma ferrem, Italiam reliqui.' at Sulla adulescentis officio collaudato omnia munera ei, quae Athenis acceperat, proficiscens iussit deferri. 3. Hic complures annos moratus, cum et rei familiari tantum operae daret quantum non indiligens deberet pater familias, et omnia reliqua tempora aut litteris aut Atheniensium rei publicae tribueret, nihilo minus amicis urbana officia praestitit. 4. nam et ad comitia eorum uentitauit et, si qua res maior acta est, non defuit. sicut Ciceroni in omnibus eius periculis singularem fidem praebuit: cui ex patria fugienti HS ducenta et quinquaginta milia donauit. 5. tranquillatis autem rebus Romanis remigrauit Romam, ut opinor L. Cotta et L. Torquato

---

[1] The explanatory gloss *quod nonnulli ita interpretantur, amitti ciuitatem Romanam alia ascita* appears in the manuscripts at this point, but has been omitted from the text.
[2] *effigies* is P. K. Marshall's emendation. The MSS have *et fidie*.
[3] *cui quidem* is an emendation. One MS has *qui*, the other *igitur* (which Nepos uses nowhere else).

consulibus. quem digredientem[1] sic uniuersa ciuitas Atheniensium prosecuta est ut lacrimis desiderii futuri dolorem indicaret.

5 Habebat auunculum Q. Caecilium, equitem Romanum, familiarem L. Luculli, diuitem, difficillima natura. cuius sic asperitatem ueritus est ut, quem nemo ferre posset, huius sine offensione ad summam senectutem retinuerit beneuolentiam. quo facto tulit pietatis fructum. 2. Caecilius enim moriens testamento adoptauit eum heredemque fecit ex dodrante. ex qua hereditate accepit circiter centies sestertium. 3. erat nupta soror Attici Q. Tullio Ciceroni, easque nuptias M. Cicero conciliarat, cum quo a condiscipulatu uiuebat coniunctissime, multo etiam familiarius quam cum Quinto, ut iudicari possit plus in amicitia ualere similitudinem morum quam affinitatem. 4. utebatur autem intime Q. Hortensio, qui iis temporibus principatum eloquentiae tenebat, ut intellegi non posset uter eum plus diligeret, Cicero an Hortensius, et (id quod erat difficillimum) efficiebat ut, inter quos tanta laudis esset aemulatio, nulla intercederet obtrectatio essetque talium uirorum copula.

6 In re publica ita est uersatus ut semper optimarum partium et esset et existimaretur, neque tamen se ciuilibus fluctibus committeret, quod non magis eos in sua potestate existimabat esse qui se his dedissent quam qui maritimis iactarentur. 2. honores non petiit, cum ei paterent propter uel gratiam uel dignitatem: quod neque peti more maiorum neque capi possent conseruatis legibus in tam effusi ambitus largitionibus neque <geri> e re publica sine periculo corruptis ciuitatis moribus. ad hastam publicam numquam accessit, (3.) nullius rei neque praes neque manceps factus est, neminem neque suo nomine neque subscribens accusauit, in ius de sua re numquam iit, iudicium nullum habuit. 4. multorum consulum praetorumque praefecturas delatas sic accepit ut neminem in prouinciam sit secutus, honore fuerit contentus, rei familiaris despexerit fructum, qui ne cum Quinto quidem Cicerone uoluerit ire in Asiam cum apud eum legati locum obtinere posset. non enim decere se arbitrabatur, cum praeturam gerere noluisset, asseclam esse praetoris. 5. qua in re non solum dignitati seruiebat, sed etiam tranquillitati, cum suspiciones quoque uitaret criminum. quo fiebat ut eius obseruantia omnibus esset

---

[1] *digredientem* is P.K. Marshall's emendation. The MSS have *diem*.

carior, cum eam officio, non timori neque spei attribui uiderent.
7 Incidit Caesarianum ciuile bellum, cum haberet annos circiter sexaginta. usus est aetatis uacatione neque se quoquam mouit ex urbe. quae amicis suis opus fuerant ad Pompeium proficiscentibus, omnia ex sua re familiari dedit, ipsum Pompeium coniunctum non offendit. 2. nullum ab eo habebat ornamentum, ut ceteri, qui per eum aut honores aut diuitias ceperant: quorum partim inuitissimi castra sunt secuti, partim summa cum eius offensione domi remanserunt. 3. Attici autem quies tantopere Caesari fuit grata ut uictor, cum priuatis pecunias per epistulas imperaret, huic non solum molestus non fuerit, sed etiam sororis filium et Q. Ciceronem ex Pompei castris concesserit. sic uetere instituto uitae effugit noua pericula.
8 Secutum est illud <tempus> occiso Caesare quo res publica penes Brutos uideretur esse et Cassium ac tota ciuitas se ad eos conuertisse. 2. sic M. Bruto usus est ut nullo ille adulescens aequali familiarius quam hoc sene, neque solum eum principem consili haberet, sed etiam in conuictu. 3. excogitatum est a quibusdam ut priuatum aerarium Caesaris interfectoribus ab equitibus Romanis constitueretur. id facile effici posse arbitrati sunt si principes eius ordinis pecunias contulissent. itaque appellatus est a C. Flauio, Bruti familiari, Atticus ut eius rei princeps esse uellet. 4. at ille, qui officia amicis praestanda sine factione existimaret semperque a talibus se consiliis remouisset, respondit: si quid Brutus <se> de suis facultatibus uti uoluisset, usurum quantum eae paterentur, sed neque cum quoquam de ea re collocuturum neque coiturum. sic ille consensionis globus huius unius dissensione disiectus est. 5. neque multo post superior esse coepit Antonius, ita ut Brutus et Cassius <destituta tutela> prouinciarum, quae iis dicis causa datae erant a consule, desperatis rebus in exilium proficiscerentur. 6. Atticus, qui pecuniam simul cum ceteris conferre noluerat florenti illi parti, abiecto Bruto Italiaque cedenti HS centum milia muneri misit. eidem in Epiro absens trecenta iussit dari, neque eo magis potenti adulatus est Antonio neque desperatos reliquit.
9 Secutum est bellum gestum apud Mutinam. in quo si tantum eum prudentem dicam, minus quam debeam praedicem, cum ille potius diuinus fuerit, si diuinatio appellanda est perpetua naturalis bonitas quae nullis casibus agitur neque minuitur. 2. hostis Antonius iudicatus Italia cesserat, spes restituendi nulla

erat. non solum inimici, qui tum erant potentissimi et plurimi, sed etiam qui aduersariis eius se dabant et in eo laedendo aliquam consecuturos sperabant commoditatem, Antoni familiares insequebantur, uxorem Fuluiam omnibus rebus spoliare cupiebant, liberos etiam exstinguere parabant. 3. Atticus, cum Ciceronis intima familiaritate uteretur, amicissimus esset Bruto, non modo nihil iis indulsit ad Antonium uiolandum, sed e contrario familiares eius ex urbe profugientes quantum potuit texit, quibus rebus indiguerunt adiuuit. 4. P. uero Volumnio ea tribuit ut plura a parente proficisci non potuerint. ipsi autem Fuluiae, cum litibus distineretur magnisque terroribus uexaretur, tanta diligentia officium suum praestitit ut nullum illa stiterit uadimonium sine Attico, sponsor omnium rerum fuerit. 5. quin etiam cum illa fundum secunda fortuna emisset in diem neque post calamitatem uersuram facere potuisset, ille se interposuit pecuniamque sine faenore sineque ulla stipulatione credidit, maximum existimans quaestum, memorem gratumque cognosci, simulque aperire se non fortunae, sed hominibus solere esse amicum. 6. quae cum faciebat, nemo eum temporis causa facere poterat existimare: nemini enim in opinionem ueniebat Antonium rerum potiturum. 7. sed †sensim is† a nonnullis optimatibus [eius] reprehendebatur quod parum odisse malos ciues uideretur. ille autem, sui iudicii <potens>, potius quid se facere par esset intuebatur quam quid alii laudaturi forent.

10 Conuersa subito fortuna est. ut Antonius rediit in Italiam, nemo non magno in periculo Atticum putarat propter intimam familiaritatem Ciceronis et Bruti. 2. itaque ad aduentum imperatorum de foro decesserat timens proscriptionem latebatque apud P. Volumnium, cui, sicut ostendimus, paulo ante opem tulerat (tanta uarietas iis temporibus fuit fortunae, ut modo hi modo illi in summo essent aut fastigio aut periculo), habebatque secum Q. Gellium Canum, aequalem simillimumque sui. 3. hoc quoque sit Attici bonitatis exemplum, quod cum eo quem puerum in ludo cognorat adeo coniuncte uixit ut ad extremam aetatem amicitia eorum creuerit. 4. Antonius autem, etsi tanto odio ferebatur in Ciceronem ut non solum ei, sed etiam omnibus eius amicis esset inimicus eosque uellet proscribere multis hortantibus, tamen Attici memor fuit officii et ei, cum requisisset ubinam esset, sua manu scripsit ne timeret statimque ad se ueniret: se eum et illius <causa> Canum de proscriptorum numero exemisse. ac

ne quod periculum incideret, quod noctu fiebat, praesidium ei misit. 5. sic Atticus in summo timore non solum sibi, sed etiam ei quem carissimum habebat praesidio fuit. neque enim suae solum a quoquam auxilium petit salutis, sed coniuncti, ut appareret nullam seiunctam sibi ab eo uelle fortunam. 6. quodsi gubernator praecipua laude fertur qui nauem ex hieme marique scopuloso seruat, cur non singularis eius existimetur prudentia qui ex tot tamque grauibus procellis ciuilibus ad incolumitatem peruenit?

11 Quibus ex malis ut se emersit, nihil aliud egit quam ut <quam> plurimis, quibus rebus posset, esset auxilio. cum proscriptos praemiis imperatorum uulgus conquireret, nemo in Epirum uenit cui res ulla defuerit, nemini non ibi perpetuo manendi potestas facta est. 2. quin etiam post proelium Philippense interitumque C. Cassi et M. Bruti L. Iulium Mocillam praetorium et filium eius Aulumque Torquatum ceterosque pari fortuna perculsos instituit tueri atque ex Epiro iis omnia Samothraciam supportari iussit. difficile est omnia persequi et non necessarium. 3. illud unum intellegi uolumus, illius liberalitatem neque temporariam neque callidam fuisse. 4. id ex ipsis rebus ac temporibus iudicari potest, quod non florentibus se uenditauit, sed afflictis semper succurrit: qui quidem Seruiliam, Bruti matrem, non minus post mortem eius quam florentem coluerit. 5. sic liberalitate utens nullas inimicitias gessit, quod neque laedebat quemquam neque, si quam iniuriam acceperat, non malebat obliuisci quam ulcisci. idem immortali memoria percepta retinebat beneficia; quae autem ipse tribuerat, tam diu meminerat, quoad ille gratus erat qui acceperat. 6. itaque hic fecit ut uere dictum uideatur:

sui cuique mores fingunt fortunam hominibus.

neque tamen ille prius fortunam quam se ipse finxit, qui cauit ne qua in re iure plecteretur.

12 His ergo rebus effecit ut M. Vipsanius Agrippa, intima familiaritate coniunctus adulescenti Caesari, cum propter suam gratiam et Caesaris potentiam nullius condicionis non haberet potestatem, potissimum eius deligeret affinitatem praeoptaretque equitis Romani filiam generosarum nuptiis. 2. atque harum nuptiarum conciliator fuit (non est enim celandum) M. Antonius, triumuir rei publicae, cuius gratia cum augere possessiones posset suas, tantum afuit a cupiditate pecuniae ut nulla in re usus sit ea nisi in deprecandis amicorum aut periculis aut incommodis. 3. quod quidem sub ipsa proscriptione perillustre fuit. nam cum L. Saufei equitis

Romani, aequalis sui, qui complures annos studio ductus philosophiae <Athenis> habitabat habebatque in Italia pretiosas possessiones, triumuiri bona uendidissent consuetudine ea qua tum res gerebantur, Attici labore atque industria factum est ut eodem nuntio Saufeius fieret certior se patrimonium amisisse et recuperasse. 4. idem L. Iulium Calidum, quem post Lucreti Catullique mortem multo elegantissimum poetam nostram tulisse aetatem uere uideor posse contendere neque minus uirum bonum optimisque artibus eruditum, post proscriptionem equitum propter magnas eius Africanas possessiones in proscriptorum numerum a P. Volumnio, praefecto fabrum Antoni, absentem relatum expediuit. 5. quod in praesenti utrum ei laboriosius an gloriosius fuerit, difficile est iudicare, quod in eorum periculis non secus absentes quam praesentes amicos Attico esse curae cognitum est.

13 Neque uero ille minus bonus pater familias habitus est quam ciuis. nam cum esset pecuniosus, nemo illo minus fuit emax, minus aedificator. neque tamen non in primis bene habitauit omnibusque optimis rebus usus est. 2. nam domum habuit in colle Quirinali Tamphilianam, ab auunculo hereditate relictam, cuius amoenitas non aedificio, sed silua constabat: ipsum enim tectum antiquitus constitutum plus salis quam sumptus habebat. in quo nihil commutauit, nisi si quid uetustate coactus est. 3. usus est familia, si utilitate iudicandum est, optima, si forma, uix mediocri. namque in ea erant pueri litteratissimi, anagnostae optimi et plurimi librarii, ut ne pedisequus quidem quisquam esset qui non utrumque horum pulchre facere posset, pari modo artifices ceteri quos cultus domesticus desiderat adprime boni. 4. neque tamen horum quemquam nisi domi natum domique factum habuit: quod est signum non solum continentiae, sed etiam diligentiae. nam et non intemperanter concupiscere, quod a plurimis uideas, continentis debet duci, et potius diligentia quam pretio parare non mediocris est industriae. 5. elegans, non magnificus, splendidus, non sumptuosus, omnique diligentia munditiam, non affluentiam affectabat. supellex modica, non multa, ut in neutram partem conspici posset. 6. nec praeteribo, quamquam nonnullis leue uisum iri putem, cum in primis lautus esset eques Romanus et non parum liberaliter domum suam omnium ordinum homines inuitaret, scimus non amplius quam terna milia peraeque in singulos menses ex ephemeride eum expensum sumptui ferre solitum. 7. atque hoc non

auditum, sed cognitum praedicamus: saepe enim propter familiaritatem domesticis rebus interfuimus.

14 Nemo in conuiuio eius aliud acroama audiuit quam anagnosten (quod nos quidem iucundissimum arbitramur), neque umquam sine aliqua lectione apud eum cenatum est, ut non minus animo quam uentre conuiuae delectarentur. 2. namque eos uocabat quorum mores a suis non abhorrerent. cum tanta pecuniae facta esset accessio, nihil de cotidiano cultu mutauit, nihil de uitae consuetudine, tantaque usus est moderatione ut neque in sestertio uicies quod a patre acceperat parum se splendide gesserit, neque in sestertio centies affluentius uixerit quam instituerat, parique fastigio steterit in utraque fortuna. 3. nullos habuit hortos, nullam suburbanam aut maritimam sumptuosam uillam, neque in Italia, praeter Arretinum et Nomentanum, rusticum praedium, omnisque eius pecuniae reditus constabat in Epiroticis et urbanis possessionibus. ex quo cognosci potest usum eum pecuniae non magnitudine, sed ratione metiri solitum.

15 Mendacium neque dicebat neque pati poterat. itaque eius comitas non sine seueritate erat neque grauitas sine facilitate, ut difficile esset intellectu utrum eum amici magis uererentur an amarent. quidquid rogabatur, religiose promittebat, quod non liberalis, sed leuis arbitrabatur polliceri quod praestare non posset. 2. idem in tuendo[1] quod semel annuisset, tanta erat cura ut non mandatam, sed suam rem uideretur agere. numquam suscepti negotii eum pertaesum est: suam enim existimationem in ea re agi putabat, qua nihil habebat carius. 3. quo fiebat ut omnia Ciceronum, M. Catonis, Q. Hortensi, Auli Torquati, multorum praeterea equitum Romanorum negotia procuraret. ex quo iudicari poterat non inertia, sed iudicio fugisse rei publicae procurationem.

16 Humanitatis uero nullum adferre maius testimonium possum quam quod adulescens idem seni Sullae fuit iucundissimus, senex adulescenti M. Bruto, cum aequalibus autem suis Q. Hortensio et M. Cicerone sic uixit ut iudicare difficile sit cui aetati fuerit aptissimus. 2. quamquam eum praecipue dilexit Cicero, ut ne frater quidem ei Quintus carior fuerit aut familiarior. 3. ei rei sunt indicio praeter eos libros in quibus de eo facit mentionem qui in uulgus sunt editi, undecim uolumina epistularum ab consulatu eius usque ad extremum

---

[1]*tuendo* is P. K. Marshall's emendation. The MSS have *nitendo*.

tempus ad Atticum missarum. quae qui legat, non multum desideret historiam contextam eorum temporum. 4. sic enim omnia de studiis principum, uitiis ducum, mutationibus rei publicae perscripta sunt ut nihil in eis non appareat, et facile existimari possit prudentiam quodam modo esse diuinationem. non enim Cicero ea solum quae uiuo se acciderunt futura praedixit, sed etiam quae nunc usu ueniunt cecinit ut uates.

17 De pietate autem Attici quid plura commemorem? cum hoc ipsum uere gloriantem audierim in funere matris suae, quam extulit annorum nonaginta, cum <complesset>[1] septem et sexaginta, se numquam cum matre in gratiam redisse, numquam cum sorore fuisse in simultate, quam prope aequalem habebat. 2. quod est signum aut nullam umquam inter eos querimoniam intercessisse aut hunc ea fuisse in suos indulgentia ut, quos amare deberet, irasci eis nefas duceret. 3. neque id fecit natura solum, quamquam omnes ei paremus, sed etiam doctrina: nam principum philosophorum ita percepta habuit praecepta ut iis ad uitam agendam, non ad ostentationem uteretur.

18 Moris etiam maiorum summus imitator fuit antiquitatisque amator, quam adeo diligenter habuit cognitam ut eam totam in eo uolumine exposuerit quo magistratus ordinauit. 2. nulla enim lex neque pax neque bellum neque res illustris est populi Romani quae non in eo suo tempore sit notata, et, quod difficillimum fuit, sic familiarum originem subtexuit ut ex eo clarorum uirorum propagines possimus cognoscere. 3. fecit hoc idem separatim in aliis libris, ut M. Bruti rogatu Iuniam familiam a stirpe ad hanc aetatem ordine enumerauerit, notans, qui a quoque ortus quos honores quibusque temporibus cepisset. 4. pari modo Marcelli Claudii [de] Marcellorum, Scipionis Cornelii et Fabii Maximi Fabiorum et Aemiliorum. quibus libris nihil potest esse dulcius iis qui aliquam cupiditatem habent notitiae clarorum uirorum. 5. attigit <artem> quoque poeticen; credimus, ne eius expers esset suauitatis. namque uersibus, qui honore rerumque gestarum amplitudine ceteros Romani populi praestiterunt, (6.) exposuit ita ut sub singulorum imaginibus facta magistratusque eorum non amplius quaternis quinisue uersibus descripserit. quod uix credendum sit tantas res tam breuiter potuisse declarari. est etiam unus liber Graece confectus, de consulatu Ciceronis.

---

[1]*complesset* is an emendation. One MS has *ipse*, the other nothing. Cf. 21.1.

19 Hactenus Attico uiuo edita a nobis sunt. nunc, quoniam fortuna nos superstites ei esse uoluit, reliqua persequemur et quantum potuerimus rerum exemplis lectores docebimus, sicut supra significauimus, suos cuique mores plerumque conciliare fortunam. 2. namque hic contentus ordine equestri quo erat ortus, in adfinitatem peruenit imperatoris Diui fili, cum iam ante familiaritatem eius esset consecutus nulla alia re quam elegantia uitae, qua ceteros ceperat principes ciuitatis dignitate pari, fortuna humiliores. 3. tanta enim prosperitas Caesarem est consecuta ut nihil ei non tribuerit fortuna quod cuiquam ante detulerit, et conciliarit quod nemo adhuc ciuis Romanus quiuit consequi. 4. nata est autem Attico neptis ex Agrippa, cui uirginem filiam collocarat. hanc Caesar uix anniculam Ti. Claudio Neroni, Drusilla nato, priuigno suo, despondit. quae coniunctio necessitudinem eorum sanxit, familiaritatem reddidit frequentiorem. (**20**.1) quamuis ante haec sponsalia non solum, cum ab urbe abesset, numquam ad suorum quemquam litteras misit quin Attico mitteret quid ageret, in primis quid legeret quibusque in locis et quamdiu esset moraturus, (2.) sed etiam, cum esset in urbe et propter infinitas suas occupationes minus saepe quam uellet Attico frueretur, nullus dies temere intercessit quo non ad eum scriberet, cum modo aliquid de antiquitate ab eo requireret, modo aliquam quaestionem poeticam ei proponeret, interdum iocans eius uerbosiores eliceret epistulas. 3. ex quo accidit, cum aedis Iouis Feretri in Capitolio ab Romulo constituta uetustate atque incuria detecta prolaberetur, ut Attici admonitu Caesar eam reficiendam curaret. 4. neque uero a M. Antonio minus absens litteris colebatur, adeo ut accurate ille ex ultimis terris quid ageret curae sibi haberet certiorem facere Atticum. 5. hoc quale sit, facilius existimabit is qui iudicare poterit quantae sit sapientiae eorum retinere usum beniuolentiamque inter quos maximarum rerum non solum aemulatio, sed etiam obtrectatio tanta intercedebat quantam fuit incidere necesse inter Caesarem atque Antonium, cum se uterque principem non solum urbis Romae, sed orbis terrarum esse cuperet.

21 Tali modo cum septem et septuaginta annos complesset atque ad extremam senectutem non minus dignitate quam gratia fortunaque creuisset (multas enim hereditates nulla alia re quam bonitate consecutus <est> tantaque prosperitate usus esset ualetudinis ut annis triginta medicina non indiguisset), (2.) nactus est morbum, quem initio et ipse et medici contempserunt: nam putarunt esse tenesmon, cui remedia celeria faciliaque proponebantur. 3. in hoc cum tres menses sine ullis doloribus praeterquam quos ex curatione capiebat consumpsisset, subito tanta uis morbi in imum intestinum prorupit ut extremo tempore per lumbos fistulae puris eruperint. 4. atque hoc priusquam ei accideret, postquam in dies dolores accrescere febresque accessisse sensit, Agrippam generum ad se accersi iussit et cum eo L. Cornelium Balbum Sextumque Peducaeum. 5. hos ut uenisse uidit, in cubitum innixus 'quantam' inquit 'curam diligentiamque in ualetudine mea tuenda hoc tempore adhibuerim, cum uos testes habeam, nihil necesse est pluribus uerbis commemorare. quibus quoniam, ut spero, satisfeci me nihil reliqui fecisse quod ad sanandum me pertineret, reliquum est ut egomet mihi consulam. id uos ignorare nolui: nam mihi stat alere morbum desinere. 6. namque his diebus quidquid cibi sumpsi, ita produxi uitam ut auxerim dolores sine spe salutis. quare a uobis peto, primum ut consilium probetis meum, deinde ne frustra dehortando impedire conemini.'

22 Hac oratione habita tanta constantia uocis atque uultus ut non ex uita, sed ex domo in domum uideretur migrare, (2.) cum quidem Agrippa eum flens atque osculans oraret atque obsecraret ne id quod natura cogeret ipse quoque sibi acceleraret letum,[1] et, quoniam tum quoque posset temporibus superesse, se sibi suisque reseruaret, preces eius taciturna sua obstinatione depressit. 3. sic cum biduum cibo se abstinuisset, subito febris decessit leuiorque morbus esse coepit. tamen propositum nihilo setius peregit. itaque die quinto postquam id consilium inierat, pridie kal. Aprilis Cn. Domitio C. Sosio consulibus decessit. 4. elatus est in lecticula, ut ipse praescripserat, sine ulla pompa funeris, comitantibus omnibus bonis, maxima uulgi frequentia. sepultus est iuxta uiam Appiam ad quintum lapidem in monumento Q. Caecilii, auunculi sui.

---

[1] *letum* is P. K. Marshall's emendation. One MS has *luctum*, the other a gap.

COMMENTARY

1.1 **stirpis** < *stirps*, f., "shoot, stock, ancestry." Some members of the Pomponian *gens* prided themselves on descent from Pompo, one of the four sons of Numa Pompilius (Romulus' successor as king of Rome).
perpetuo: "always"; an adverb, to be taken with *obtinuit* ("retained, kept"). The peculiar placement of the adverb (at a distance from its verb) lends it emphasis; Nepos means us to understand that Atticus could have risen to senatorial rank, had he wanted to. He returns to the theme in 19.2.

1.2 **patre usus est diligente:** "he had an attentive father." The expression puts the emphasis on the modifier; *usus est* < *utor*, regularly constructed with the ablative.
ut tum erant tempora: "for those times." The *ut*-clause limits the compass of the adjectives *diti* ("wealthy") and *studioso litterarum* ("scholarly").
inprimis: "particularly, especially"; a fossilized adverbial expression.
prout: "just as, insofar as."
impertiri < *impertio*, "give a share to, impart" + dative; in the passive, "be given over to" + dative.

1.3 **erat:** "there was." When a form of *esse* appears first in its clause it is usually to be translated thus.
ut ... acciperet: adverbial result clause. There is no adverb in the main clause to indicate that this is a clause of result (rather than, e.g., purpose), but the sense of the passage requires it. See below on 1.4 *ut ... fuerit*. The second verb of the clause, *pronuntiaret* ("recited"), is connected to *acciperet* by *non solum ... sed etiam*, "not only ... but also."
qua ex re: "and as a result," literally "and from this thing." *qua*, a connecting relative pronoun, is most easily translated as if it were *et ea*.
nobilis: "remarkable." The adjective is derived from *notare*, "to mark."
clariusque exsplendescebat quam <ut> ... condiscipuli ... possent: "and he was so splendidly brilliant that his fellow students could not," literally "and he was more splendidly brilliant than that his fellow students could." <ut >... *possent* is an adverbial result clause that defines the sense of the adverbial expression *clarius ... quam*, just as in the last sentence in §1 the clause *ut ... carior* defines the sense of the adverb *sic*. See AG 535a, 571a. The pointed brackets indicate letters or words that have to be supplied in the text, though they are absent in the manuscript tradition.
generosi: "well-born."
animo aequo: "unmoved," literally "with feelings level"; ablative of manner. Nepos means this in a positive sense: Atticus' fellow students were stimulated by his example.

1.4 **suo:** direct reflexive, i.e., one referring to the subject of the clause in which it appears. Contrast on 2.2 *sibi*.
L. Torquatus: Born c. 108, in Sulla's train after the sack of Athens in 86, he reached the consulship in 65.

C. Marius filius: son of the like-named famous Marius (cos. 107, 104-100, 86) and Julius Caesar's aunt, Julia. Born c. 110 BC (the same year as Atticus), he was consul in 82, and died fighting Sulla's forces in that year. Note that Sullan and anti-Sullan appear side-by-side among Atticus' friends. Atticus made himself useful to individuals on both sides of this conflict, and he would do the same in the next two rounds of civil wars (see 7.1 and 8.1).
M. Cicero: the famous orator, consul of 63. He was some four years younger than Atticus. The education of these young men was supervised by the eminent orator L. Crassus. See Cicero, *de Oratore* 2.2 for a description of the process.
consuetudine: "companionship."
ut ... fuerit: adverbial result clause. Such clauses are often, as here, signalled by an adverb such as *sic*, *tantum*, *tam* or the like. The "sequence of tenses" rule would seem to require a secondary tense in this clause, but the perfect subjunctive is used to indicate that the result was not only logical, but actual. See AG 485c.
nemo ... perpetuo: "never anyone," literally "always no one."
iis: dative.

2.1 **mature:** "at an early age."
affinitatem: "relationship by marriage."
P. Sulpici: Tribune of the plebs in 88, he tried to enact a program of reform against the wishes of the optimate party (see on 6.1 *optimarum partium*). He won the support of Marius (the father) by transferring to him an important military command which the senate had previously assigned to Sulla, and was killed as a result of Sulla's vengeful march on Rome in 88.
pl.: abbreviation for *plebis*. *Tribunus plebis* is predicative here: "while tribune of the plebs."
expers: "without a part in" + genitive.
illius: Sulpicius'.
consobrina: "daughter of his mother's sister."
nupserat < *nubo*, "be married to" + dative.

2.2 **Cinnano tumultu:** "the upheavals involving Cinna," i.e., in the period 87-84, in which L. Cornelius Cinna held 4 consulships, was deposed once (87), tried to restore orderly government, began a military campaign and was killed in a mutiny.
ciuitatem esse perturbatam: indirect statement after *uidit*.
sibi: indirect reflexive, i.e., one referring not to the subject of the clause in which it appears (the subject of accusative/infinitive clause in which *sibi* appears is *facultatem*) but to the subject of the clause on which its clause depends (here, to Atticus, the subject of *uidit*). Contrast on 1.4 *suo*.
facultatem ... uiuendi: "opportunity of living." The gerund is a defining genitive.
pro dignitate: "as was appropriate to his status."

quin ... offenderet: "without offending," literally "how he might not offend." *quin* is a compressed form of *qui* (the old ablative of the relative pronoun, meaning "how") and the negative conjunction *ne*.
alterutram partem: "one side or the other."
dissociatis animis: ablative absolute.
cum ... fauerent partibus: causal. *faueo*, "favor, support" + dative.
Sullanis: The "party" of L. Cornelius Sulla Felix (the optimates, see on 6.1 *optimarum partium*) was ultimately victorious, but endured heavy weather from the party of Marius and Cinna while Sulla was in the East fighting Mithridates (88-84).
idoneum tempus: sc. *esse*; indirect statement after *ratus* (< *reor*, "think").
studiis obsequendi suis: "of pursuing his studies." *obsequendi* ("pursue" + dative) is a defining genitive to be taken with *tempus*.
Athenas: The Latin name for Athens is feminine and plural in form, *Athenae*.
se contulit: "took himself"; this is the main clause of this long and wandering sentence. Atticus remained based in Greece until the mid 60s, when he returned to Rome in time to help Cicero win the consulship of 63.
neque eo setius: "nonetheless," literally "and not less (*setius*) by this (*eo*)."
adulescentem Marium: See on 1.4 *C. Marius filius*. The man was in fact an unusually (and illegally) young consul in 82, being only 28 years of age (the legal age was 42).
hostem iudicatum: "when he had been adjudged an enemy [of the state]." Sulla outlawed the young Marius in 82 by placing his name (together with those of some 4700 other Romans) on the proscription lists. The property of those proscribed was forfeit to the state and they could be killed with impunity. Marius was killed by Sullan troops in 82.
opibus suis: "with his own resources"; *opibus* < *ops*. The reflexive *suis* emphasizes the risk Atticus took in contributing materially to the losing cause in a very bitter civil war.
cuius: Marius'.

2.3 **ne ... afferret:** negative purpose clause.
rei familiari: "to his net worth," literally "to his family property."
eodem: "to the same place," i.e., "to Athens."
hic: "here."
uixit < *uiuo*, "live."

2.4 **iam:** "already."
uersuram facere publice: "to refinance the city's loans." A *uersura* is an exchange; in this expression, an exchange of one creditor for another. *Publice* is an adverb used for official business.
eius: sc. *uersurae*.
condicionem: "terms."
haberent: The subject is *Athenienses*.

ut neque ... acceperit neque ... passus sit: adverbial result clause. See on 1.4 *ut ... fuerit* for the perfect subjunctives.
usuram: "interest," literally "a fee for use [of money]."
quam dictum esset: comparative clause. The verb is attracted into the subjunctive mood by the subjunctives that surround it. The pluperfect tense is used because a secondary sequence tense is required after *interposuit*.
debere: "to owe."

2.5 **quod utrumque:** "and each of these things, both things."
neque ... inueterascere ... aes alienum patiebatur neque ... crescere: "he allowed their debt neither to grow old nor to increase." *patiebatur* has two complementary infinitives, and the subject of both is *aes alienum* "debt" (literally "someone else's bronze").
multiplicandis usuris: "by allowing the interest to compound." The phrase is parallel to *indulgendo*, but a gerundive rather than a gerund. Nepos could have used the gerund *multiplicando* with a direct object *usuras*, but classical authors tended to replace the gerund + direct object construction with the passive gerundive.

2.6 **auxit** < *augeo*, "increase."
donauit: "presented with" + accusative of the recipient and ablative of the gift.
seni modii: "six modii each." The *modius* was a Roman dry measure, about 2 gallons in quantity. *seni*, "six each," is a distributive numeral, and is adjectival in form (*seni, -ae, -a* etc.)
tritici: "wheat"; partitive genitive.
medimnus: a Greek dry measure equivalent, as Nepos says, to six *modii*.

3.1 **Hic:** "here."
se gerebat: "he conducted himself."
communis: "common to, at home among" + dative.
infimis: "the lowest [ranks of society]." *infimus* and *imus* (see in 21.3) are alternative forms of the superlative of *inferus*, "below."
quo factum est: "and so it happened that" + substantive result clause (*ut ... omnes honores haberent*, "rewarded in every way"). See AG 568.
haberent: The subject is *Athenienses*.

3.2 **ne qua sibi statua poneretur restitit:** "he resisted [having] any statue put up in his honor (*sibi*)." *restitit* introduces a clause of prevention (see AG 558b). *qua* < *qui*, "any." The indefinite adjective *qui* and the indefinite pronoun *quis* are used instead of *aliqui* and *aliquis* after *si, nisi, num* and *ne* (see AG 310a).
aliquot: "several"; an indeclinable number word.

3.3 **cui ... primum illud munus fortunae:** sc. *erat*, "for whom, first of all, that was a gift of fortune." *primum* is an adverb. *illud* looks forward to *hoc* below. *fortunae* is a subjective genitive.
quod ... natus est: "that he was born"; substantive *quod*-clause in apposition to *illud*. See AG 572.

in ea potissimum urbe: "in that city, above all." The adverb *potissimum* emphasizes *ea* and prepares the way for the relative clause which explains why *ea urbs* was unique.
in qua ... esset: relative clause of characteristic. See AG 535b.
orbis terrarum: "the world." *orbis* is an objective genitive dependent on *imperi*.
hoc specimen prudentiae: sc. *erat*, "...[whereas] this was evidence of his intellectual powers." *hoc* picks us the construction initiated by *illud* above; the pronouns help articulate the contrast between what Atticus owes to chance and what he owes to his own character. In English, "whereas" make the contrast clearer. *specimen*, "a sign, evidence."
quod ... fuit carissimus: "that he was very dear"; substantive *quod*-clause, in apposition to *hoc*.
se ... contulisset: See on 2.2 *se contulit*.

4.1 ex Asia Sulla decedens: In 84, after having made Mithridates an ally of the *populus Romanus*, Sulla rebelled from the government of Cinna and invaded Italy. A bloody civil war ensued, one in which Atticus refused to take an active part.
secum: With pronouns the preposition *cum* tends to follow and to be attached—*secum, mecum, tecum, nobiscum, quocum* etc.
leporem < *lepos*, "charm."
ascitum < *ascisco*, "acquire."
poemata < *poema*, "poem." Nepos uses a Greek accusative neuter plural ending for this Greek word.

4.2 factum est: For the construction, see on 3.1 *quo factum est*.
noli ... uelle: "don't desire"; a form of prohibition. Neither syntax nor word order indicates whether *me* is the subject or the object of *ducere*, but sense requires that it be the object. This is one of only two bits of direct "quotation" in the *Life* (for the other, see §21). With this device Nepos highlights two characteristic (and praiseworthy) moments in his subject's life, a declaration of neutrality (here) and a demonstration of firm reliance on his own judgement (in §21).
cum quibus ... reliqui: It is difficult to put this portion of the sentence directly into English. The best approach is to begin a new sentence here. Start with the main clause *Italiam reliqui*, then add the negative purpose clause *ne ... ferrem*, then translate the phrase *cum quibus* as a demonstrative, "with them."

4.3 Hic: "here."
complures annos: accusative of duration.
cum ... daret: concessive. The concessive use of *cum* is often signalled by the presence of a strong negative (such as *nihilo minus* here) or a word like *tamen* at the start of the main clause.
tantum operae ... quantum: "as much effort ... as." *operae* is a partitive genitive. *tantum* and *quantum* are correlatives; the presence of the first term signals that the second will be along soon. By means of such devices Latin speakers guide their audiences through their sometimes lengthy sentences.

familias: an archaic form of the genitive singular (compare the genitive singular ending of the Greek first declension), which survived in a few expressions only: in addition to this one, also *mater familias* and *filius familias*.

Atheniensium rei publicae: Here *res publica*, often used to refer to the Roman state, retains its original sense of "public affairs."

urbana officia praestitit: "rendered services in the city [of Rome]."

4.4 **comitia:** "elections."

uentitauit < *uentito*, "make a habit of coming"; a frequentative verb derived from *uenio*.

maior: "rather important."

Ciceroni in omnibus eius periculis: Cicero's *pericula* resulted from his vigorous suppression of the Catilinarian conspiracy while consul in 63. He had some of the leading conspirators executed without trial, and was in danger thereafter of being brought to trial himself. He spent a year and a half in exile in 58-57 to avoid just this.

fugienti: "going into exile." The date is March 58.

HS: a symbol meaning "sesterces," a contraction of *semis-tertius*. The original value of a sestertius was two and one half *asses* ("the third [*as*] is a half"). The symbol is a corruption of IIS ("two" and "half" [*semis*]). With the sum mentioned (250,000 HS), one may compare the yearly allowance of 80,000 HS that Cicero gave his son when he was studying in Athens. This was deemed an ample stipend (*Letters to Atticus* 16.1.5).

donauit: "gave"; here with the accusative of the gift and dative of the recipient. Contrast on 2.6 *donauit*.

4.5 **L. Cotta et L. Torquato consulibus:** "in the consulship of Cotta and Torquatus"; ablative absolute. The year is 65 B.C.

digredientem: predicative, "while he was departing."

prosecuta est < *prosequor*, "escort."

desiderii futuri: "of being without him in the future," literally "of their future longing [for him]."

5.1 **Q. Caecilium:** A wealthy member of the equestrian order, he made his money and his reputation for harshness as a money-lender (viz. banker). He seems also to have served as a business agent for L. Lucullus (see below). Caecilius died in 58.

L. Luculli: the general who fought for many years (73-66) against Mithridates, only to have credit for the final victory snatched from him by Pompey. He retired from public life thereafter, and cultivated his fishponds. Nepos mentions Lucullus here because he had been thought the most likely recipient of the estate of the childless Q. Caecilius (see Valerius Maximus 7.8.5).

difficillima natura: ablative of description.

asperitatem ueritus est: "respected [Caecilius'] irritability." *ueritus est* < *uereor*.

ut ... retinuerit: For the force of the perfect subjunctive, see on 1.4 *ut ... fuerit*.

quem ... posset: "and although no one [else] could bear him"; concessive relative clause. *quem* refers to Q. Caecilius.
5.2 heredem ... ex dodrante: "heir to three-quarters of his property."
centies sestertium: By convention, the multiplier *centena milia* (100,000) is omitted from large sums of money. Atticus' inheritance amounted to 100 times (*centies*) one hundred thousand sesterces, or 10 million sesterces. (*Sestertium* is a partitive genitive.)
5.3 conciliarat = *conciliauerat*, "had brought about."
Q. Tullio Ciceroni: the younger brother of the famous Cicero, Marcus. Quintus followed his brother up the *cursus honorum* (the political career ladder) as far as the praetorship, but was never consul. He served under Julius Caesar in Gaul (see, e.g., Caesar's *Bellum Gallicum* 5.38-52). His marriage to Atticus' sister Pomponia was not a happy one.
uiuebat: Atticus is the subject.
multo ... familiarius: "much more intimately," literally "more intimately by much."
ut ... possit: adverbial result clause in secondary sequence (after *uiuebat*), but with a present subjunctive because the author wants to impress upon us the fact that the result is still felt in the present. Contrast this with the result clause in the next sentence: *utebatur intime Q. Hortensio ... ut intellegi non posset uter eum plus diligeret*, which refers to a question Atticus' *contemporaries* may have been asking themselves.
ualere similitudinem: indirect statement functioning as the "subject" of the impersonal expression *iudicari possit*. Literally, "that similarity of character matters more ... can be judged," but "one may judge that similarity of character matters more" is a less awkward equivalent.
morum < *mos*, "habit"; in the plural, "character."
5.4 Q. Hortensio: the leading orator in Rome before Cicero made a name for himself by winning his case against Hortensius' client Verres (70 BC). Hortensius was a staunch optimate and became consul in 69.
uter ... plus diligeret: "which [of the two] was more fond of"; indirect question functioning as the "subject" of the impersonal expression *intellegi non posset*.
aemulatio: "rivalry."
ut ... intercederet: substantive result clause, functioning as the "object" of *efficiebat*. See on 3.1 *quo factum est* for a passive version of this sort of expression.
obtrectatio: "[unseemly] conflict."
essetque copula: "there was a bond." See on 1.3 *erat*.
6.1 est uersatus < *uersor*, "be involved."
optimarum partium: "of the optimate party." Roman political "parties" were extremely fluid. The safest generalization is that the *optimates* (to which Nepos refers with the adjective *optimarum*) were associated with the desire of the Senate to run things for the benefit first and foremost of the senatorial class, whereas *populares* proclaimed that the Senate ought to run things in such a way that the *populus Romanus* was

the first beneficiary. These labels were often used in name-calling or in self-advertisement, hence Nepos' phrase *et esset et existimaretur*.
neque = *et non*. It joins *committeret* to the *ut*-clause.
ciuilibus fluctibus: "political turbulence." The metaphor of the waves on which the ship of state is tossed was already so old that Nepos does not qualify it (with *quidam* or *ut ita dicam*).
quod ... existimabat: causal *quod*-clause, with an indicative verb, meaning that the author is vouching for Atticus' reasoning. If he had said *quod existimaret*, he would have been reporting Atticus' thoughts without passing judgement on their validity.
eos: accusative subject of the indirect statement and antecedent of *qui ... dedissent*.
sua: direct reflexive, referring to *eos*.
qui ... dedissent ... qui ... iactarentur: Relative clauses generally have subjunctive verbs when they are contained within an indirect statement.
maritimis: sc. *fluctibus*.

6.2 **honores:** "political offices."
cum ... paterent: concessive.
quod ... possent: By using the subjunctive Nepos is limiting himself to reporting Atticus' reasoning, without expressing his own agreement (or disagreement). Contrast 6.1 *quod ... existimabat*.
conseruatis legibus: "without breaking the law."
in tam effusi ambitus largitionibus: "in the wholesale briberies of such widespread electoral corruption." *effusi* < *effundo*, "spread out."
<geri>: See on 1.3 *clariusque exsplendescebat* for the meaning of the pointed brackets.
e re publica: "Constitutionally" is a reasonable translation, provided one remembers that for the Romans the political constitution was to a large extent "the way things have been done."
ad hastam publicam ... accessit: One "approached the public spear" in order to bid on the contracts (e.g. for public works and tax collection) offered by the censors. The tax-farmers (*publicani*) had a particularly bad reputation for making personal profit out of provincial misery. See Livy 39.44.8 and 43.16.2 for descriptions of the bidding procedure.

6.3 **praes:** "guarantor"; the guarantor's property was given as security for the performance of a contract. The topic of this chapter is Atticus' involvement in public affairs, and Nepos refers here and in the preceding sentence to Atticus' avoidance of public-works contracts and tax-farming, profitable business-ventures in which many wealthy Roman knights of the day engaged.
manceps: "bidder"; the bidder conducted the negotiations for a contract, and presumably managed the business thereafter.
subscribens: Roman prosecutors were often joined by *subscriptores* who lent their authority to his case.
in ius ... iit: "went to court."

iudicium nullum habuit: "never served as a judge." Civil cases had a two-part procedure; the first (*in iure*) where the parties appeared before the praetor who would define the points at issue in the case and appoint a judge to hear the arguments and make a ruling in the second phase, the *iudicium*. There was no appeal from the ruling of these judges, and Atticus never accepted any such assignment.

6.4 delatas < *defero*, "offer."
praefecturas ... sic accepit ut neminem in prouinciam sit secutus: "he accepted the prefectures, but accompanied no one to his province." In other words, he accepted the title of "prefect," which was a mark of honor, but did not perform the functions of a prefect, which might have been profitable. *praefecti* were government officials with no particular tasks; they tended to use the public resources available to them by virtue of their position to promote personal aims. The adverbial result clause here limits the main verb. See AG 537.2b.
fructum: "profit."
qui ... uoluerit: "since ... he was willing"; causal relative clause, giving the particular decision which underlies the generalization *rei familiaris despexerit fructum*.
ne ... quidem: "not even."
in Asiam: Q. Cicero was governor of Asia in 61-59, after his praetorship (62).
cum ... posset: concessive.
non ... decere se: "that it was not suitable for him"; indirect statement dependent on *arbitrabatur*. The meaning of "it" is defined by the next accusative/infinitive phrase *asseclam esse*, "to be a hanger-on." *Assecla*, like *agricola* and *poeta*, is a masculine noun of the first declension.

6.5 seruiebat < *seruio*, "serve, be of service to" + dative.
quo fiebat ut ... esset: See on 3.1 *quo factum est. fiebat* < *fio*, "be made."
eius obseruantia: "his regard." *eius* is a subjective genitive.

7.1 cum haberet annos circiter sexaginta: The year is 49 BC, the *bellum* is that between Julius Caesar and Pompey. Atticus was in fact precisely 60.
aetatis uacatione: "the exemption [from military service] due to his age."
quoquam: "to any place."
quae amicis suis opus fuerant: "the things his friends needed." The nominative is used with *opus esse* when the thing or things needed are expressed by a neuter pronoun. See AG 411b.
coniunctum: "[although] close."

7.2 ab eo: "from Pompey."
quorum partim: "and some of them." *partim* is an adverb meaning "by parts." *quorum* is a partitive genitive.
domi: locative, to indicate place where.

7.3 uictor: predicative.

priuatis: "private citizens"; dative of disadvantage.
imperaret < *impero*, "requisition" + accusative of the object and dative of the person from whom it is sought.
sororis filium: the younger Q. Cicero, born to Atticus' sister Pomponia and Q. Cicero the elder in 66.
concesserit: "yielded." The date is 47. Atticus' involvement in the pardons secured by Quintus and his son is not attested in Cicero's correspondence on the matter (e.g. *Letters to Atticus* 11.7.7, 11.8.2, 11.9.2).

8.1 **<tempus>:** For the supplement to the text, cf. *illud tempus exspectandum ... quo*, Nepos, *Life of Alcibiades* 4.2.
penes Brutos ... et Cassium: "in the possession of the two Brutuses and Cassius." The "two Brutuses" are Decimus Iunius Brutus Albinus and Marcus Iunius Brutus; "Cassius" is Gaius Cassius Longinus. All three were tyrannicides and important figures in the fight against M. Antonius after the Ides of March, 44 BC. Actually, the tyrannicides (or liberators, depending on your politics) were never in control of public affairs, but only they ever offered a hope of restoring the constitution (the *res publica*).

8.2 **sic M. Bruto usus est:** i.e., "his relationship with M. Brutus was such" + adverbial result clause. Atticus' association with Brutus (born c. 85) is attested in Cicero's correspondence as far back as 51.
ut: sc. *usus esset*. This verb is omitted from the result clause because it can be supplied from the main verb.
nullo ... aequali: "no contemporary"; ablative with [*usus esset*].
quam hoc sene: sc. *usus est*. This verb is omitted from the comparative clause because it can be supplied from the main verb.
principem consili: "chief of his council"; the genitive is partitive. Roman men often consulted with a *consilium* of close friends before making important decisions. *principem* is also to be taken with *in conuictu* ("in his social life"); *consilium* and *in conuictu* form a doublet which covers both business and relaxation.

8.3 **excogitatum est a quibusdam:** "some people came up with a plan," literally "it was planned by some"; impersonal passive. The meaning of "it" is defined by *ut ... constitueretur*. The verb *excogito* has a rather negative flavor.
ut ... aerarium ... constitueretur: "that a fund be established"; substantive result clause functioning as the "subject" of the impersonal expression *excogitatum est*.
si ... contulissent: the protasis of a future more-vivid condition in indirect statement. What the planners thought was this: if the foremost *equites* will contribute money, it will be easy to create a fund. In direct statement, the if-clause (protasis) would use a future perfect indicative, and the main clause (apodosis) a future indicative. In indirect statement in secondary sequence the future perfect indicative is rendered by the pluperfect subjunctive. See AG 589a3. The future indicative of the main clause would normally be rendered by a future infinitive, but the present

infinitive *posse* has a future-oriented meaning and can be used instead of a proper future infinitive. See AG 516d.

C. Flauio, Bruti familiari: This man, a Roman *eques* and man of business, served Brutus as *praefectus fabrum* (roughly, aide-de-camp), and fell shortly before his friend at the battle of Philippi. See on 12.4 *praefecto fabrum*.

eius rei princeps esse: "to be the principal in this matter."

8.4 **qui ... existimaret:** relative clause with a causal flavor, hence the subjunctive verb.

officia ... praestanda: sc. *esse*, "that services should be provided."

sine factione: "regardless of what side [they were on], without taking sides."

si quid Brutus <se> de suis facultatibus uti uoluisset: "if Brutus wanted him (i.e., Atticus) to put any of his resources to use." See on 8.3 *si ... contulissent* for the tense of *uoluisset*. The accusative/infinitive *<se> ... uti* completes the sense of *uoluisset* (see AG 563b2). *<se>* is an indirect reflexive, referring to Atticus. *uti < utor*, which has here an accusative complement (*quid*), a construction which fell out of use in the classical period. See AG 410 n.1.

usurum: sc. *esse*, i.e., "he [Atticus] would use them."

quantum eae paterentur: "as far as they allowed." *paterentur < patior*. The antecedent for this relative clause, *tantum*, is omitted. See on 4.3 *tantum operae ... quantum*.

sed neque cum quoquam de ea re collocuturum neque coiturum: "but would neither discuss [the project] with anyone nor go in with anyone on it." The construction of *usurum* continues in these two future infinitives. Atticus was willing to give money to his friend, *qua* friend, but would not make a public expression of support for the cause of which Brutus was a figurehead.

ille consensionis globus: "that pack of plotters." *consensionis < consensio*, "agreement, conspiracy," a term which amplifies the negative tone already present in *excogitatum est*. Nepos is unusually vehement here.

8.5 **<destituta tutela> prouinciarum:** "the duties of government having been laid aside." In June of 44 Brutus and Cassius were given the task of supervising grain shipments from Asia and Sicily respectively (the term *prouincia* is used of such assignments as well as of territorial commands). Neither man discharged his task, and later in the summer of 44 they were assigned by the senate to the governorships of Cyrenaica (in N. Africa) and Crete. They not not go to these (insignificant) provinces either, but rather to areas more fertile in money and military forces, Cassius to Syria, Brutus to Macedonia.

dicis causa: "for form's sake"; a fossilized phrase. *dicis* is genitive; the word occurs in no other form. The preposition *causa* is post-positive, that is, it follows the word it governs (a genitive). As *praetor urbanus* and *praetor peregrinus* for 44 BC Brutus and Cassius had official duties in Rome. These they could not perform, since the tyrannicides had left

Rome in April to avoid the hostility of the populace. Their absence was "excused" by the assignment of other official tasks (*prouinciae*). See note above.
a consule: M. Antonius. Caesar had been the other regular consul of 44. Cicero's son-in-law Dolabella had been chosen by Caesar to take his place when he (Caesar) left for a foreign war; Dolabella became suffect consul after Caesar's assassination, instead. The provincial assignments were Antony's concern, however (cf. Cicero, *Letters to Atticus* 15.5.2).
in exilium: Nepos is describing the way the rather precipitate departure of Brutus and Cassius looked, and perhaps how it felt, but not a legal sentence. It was not until the latter half of 43 that the conspirators were condemned (in absentia) under the *lex Pedia*.

8.6 **florenti illi parti:** "to that side when it was strong."
abiecto Bruto: dative.
Italiaque cedenti: September, 44.
muneri: dative of purpose, coupled, as often, with a dative of reference (*Bruto*).
in Epiro absens: Atticus spent much time on his large estate in Epirus, particularly when times were troubled. His position, as friend of Brutus and diplomatically polite to Antony, was very ticklish in 44 and 43.
neque eo magis: "no more," literally "not more because of this." See on 2.2 *neque eo setius*. Here "this" represents the circumstances of Antony's rise to power and Brutus' retreat.
adulatus est < *adulor*, "fawn on, behave ingratiatingly towards," here + dative.

9.1 **bellum ... apud Mutinam:** This phase of the civil wars ranged the Caesarian Antony against Decimus Brutus, who claimed to be fighting for the constitution, the *res publica*. Caesar's heir Octavian eventually came to the aid of D. Brutus, and Antony was defeated at Mutina on 21 April in 43.
tantum: used here in its limiting sense, "only."
diuinatio: "godliness." This noun stands in the predicate, while *perpetua naturalis bonitas* is the subject of the clause.
casibus: "[ill-]fortune."

9.2 **hostis Antonius iudicatus:** This condemnation followed closely on his defeat at Mutina.
in eo laedendo: "in harming him." For the construction, see on 2.4 *multiplicandis usuris*.
se ... consecuturos: sc. *esse*, "that they would gain." The accusative and future infinitive are normal after verbs of hoping.
commoditatem: "material advantage"; postponed to the end of its clause for its shock value.
insequebantur ... cupiebant ... parabant: There are no connectives joining the three main verbs of this sentence. Asyndeton allows an author to communicate the most information in the least time, and helps Nepos convey his eagerness to communicate this information.

Fuluiam: Antony was her third husband; she had earlier been married to the fiery P. Clodius Pulcher (died 52) and the erratic C. Curio (died 49).
omnibus rebus spoliare: "to deprive of all her possessions." *rebus* is an ablative of separation.
liberos ... exstinguere parabant: Antony had three children at this point, one daughter by his first marriage, and two sons with Fulvia; in fact none was killed in 43, but Octavian did have Antony's elder son executed after the battle of Actium in 31. The metaphorical use of *exstinguere*, while not uncommon in Latin, emphasizes the regrettability of the (planned) killing by evoking the image of a light shining brightly in the darkness but suddenly put out.

9.3 **cum ... uteretur, ... esset:** concessive.
Ciceronis intima familiaritate: Cicero and Brutus supported the constitutional or Republican cause in the civil war against Antony, and Cicero called for Antony's execution on numerous occasions.
nihil iis indulsit: *indulsit* < *indulgeo*, "yield to" + dative. *nihil* is an adverbial or internal accusative, "not at all."
ad Antonium uiolandum: "for harming Antony." *ad* + gerundive expresses purpose. See AG 506.
quantum potuit, texit: *texit* < *tego*, "cover, protect." The relative clause modifies a correlative antecedent which has been omitted: *quantum potuit, [tantum] texit.* See on 4.3 *tantum operae ... quantum.*
quibus rebus indiguerunt, adiuuit: "he supplied them with the things they needed." *indiguerunt* < *indigeo*, "lack" + ablative. The expression is compressed here; the full form is *iis rebus adiuuit, quibus indiguerunt.* See AG 307e.

9.4 **P. uero Volumnio:** "in fact, in the case of P. Volumnius." *uero* signals an illustration of the generalization he has just given. The man's full name was P. Volumnius Eutrapelus ("the wit"). An *eques*, he is attested on friendly terms with Atticus' friend Cicero in 52 and 46, but served on Antony's side in 43. See on 12.4 *praefecto fabrum.*
ea tribuit: "did so much for." *ea* triggers the result clause that follows.
proficisci < *proficiscor*, "come forth, emanate."
litibus distineretur: "was distracted by lawsuits"; the subject is Fulvia. *litibus* < *lis*, "dispute, lawsuit."
nullum ... stiterit uadimonium: "appeared for no summons." *stiterit* < *sisto.*
sponsor omnium rerum: "backer in all matters [legal and financial]." Atticus is the subject.

9.5 **quin etiam:** "indeed." Introduces a specific example of the behavior he has just described.
fundum ... emisset in diem: "had bought a piece of land on credit." *emisset* < *emo.*
uersuram: "an exchange of creditors." See on 2.4 *uersuram facere publice.* Fulvia wanted to get a new loan to pay off the old debt.
faenore < *faenus*, "interest."

stipulatione: A *stipulatio* was a legally enforceable promise, a contract in effect.

maximum ... quaestum: sc. *esse*, "that it was the best [sort of] profit"; indirect statement dependent on *existimans*.

memorem ... cognosci: This phrase and the following infinitive *aperire* define what, in Atticus' estimation, was the best sort of return on an investment (*maximum quaestum esse*): "to be recognized as remembering and requiting [favors]" and "to show that he was accustomed to be the friend etc."

9.6 **temporis causa:** "thinking that times would change," literally "for the sake of the times."

nemini ... in opinionem veniebat: "it occurred to no one."

Antonium ... potiturum: sc. *esse*. *potiturum* < *potior*, "get control of," here + genitive.

9.7 **†sensim is†:** The crosses are used to mark a crux, a spot where the manuscripts are manifestly corrupt but for which no satisfactory emendation has been found. *sensim* ("gradually") does not fit the context very well, the use of *is* to indicate a change of subject is unlike Nepos' casual practice elsewhere (see on 2.4 *haberent*, 3.1 *haberent*, 5.3 *uiuebat* and 9.4 *litibus distineretur* for unmarked changes of subject), and no emendation proposed so far has accounted for *eius* (see below). The syntax of this sentence is complete without whatever was where *sensim is* is now; in translating, it may be provisionally ignored.

nonnullis: "some," literally "not none."

[eius]: Square brackets surround a word which is present in the manuscripts but which needs to be excised.

quod ... uideretur: causal *quod*-clause, reporting the reasoning of those who reproached Atticus.

sui iudicii <potens>: "able to judge for himself." For the genitive with adjectives, see AG 349a-b.

potius ... intuebatur: "he kept his sights fixed on ... rather than on ..."

quid ... par esset ... quid ... laudaturi forent: indirect questions dependent on *intuebatur*. *laudaturi forent* (= *laudaturi essent*) is a periphrastic form used in secondary sequence indirect questions to convey futurity.

10.1 **ut ... rediit:** temporal *ut*-clause. See AG 543. The date is November 43, after the formation of the Second Triumvirate (Antony, Octavian, Lepidus). More than 100 senators and many *equites* were proscribed at this time, among them Cicero and his brother and nephew, but not Atticus.

Atticum: sc. *esse*.

putarat = *putauerat*.

10.2 **ad aduentum:** "near the time of the arrival."

modo hi modo illi: "sometimes one side, sometimes the other."

summo ... fastigio: "on the highest peak [of prosperity]."

Q. Gellium Canum: This man appears briefly in Cicero's correspondence (*Letters to Atticus* 13.31.4) and may have been the father of the Cana who is mentioned in 45 as a potential wife for Atticus' nephew Quintus.
simillimumque sui: "extremely like him." *sui* is a direct reflexive, referring to Atticus. *similis* is used with the genitive of pronouns and names, the dative of nouns.

10.3 **eo:** Q. Gellius Canus.
puerum: predicative.
cognorat = *cognouerat*.
creuerit < *cresco*, "grow, increase."

10.4 **multis hortantibus:** With this ablative absolute Nepos gives us a picture of just how terrible these times were.
Attici ... officii: For instances of Atticus' service, see 9.4-7.
requisisset < *requiro*, "inquire." Antony is the subject.
ubinam esset: indirect question. Atticus is the subject. *nam* is an interrogative particle attached to *ubi*, "where?"
sua manu: another sign of the perils of the times; he wanted to ensure that Atticus did not fear a trap.
ne timeret: negative purpose clause; the subject is Atticus.
ad se: indirect reflexive, referring to Antony.
se ... exemisse: indirect statement (notice the colon) of what Antony put in his letter. *exemisse* < *eximo*, "remove."
illius <causa>: "for his (i.e., Atticus') sake."
ne quod: See on 3.2 *ne qua sibi statua poneretur, restitit*.
noctu: "at night."

10.5 **ei ... praesidio:** datives of reference and purpose.
ut appareret ... uelle: "so that it was apparent that [he] wanted." The presence of *ut* and the negative word *nullam* show that this is a result clause.
coniuncti: This word, like *suae*, goes with *salutis* ("the well-being of his friend"). You will often find possessive adjectives and genitives in tandem.
nullam seiunctam sibi ab eo ... fortunam: "no [good-]fortune for himself in which Canus did not share," more literally "that was separate from him [Canus]." *sibi* intrudes between *seiunctam* and *ab eo*, which go together. Unemphatic pronouns (such as *sibi* here) are often enclitic ("leaning on") to emphatic words in their clause, lending them weight and duration.

10.6 **quodsi:** "and as to that, if."
gubernator: "ship's pilot"; the most responsible office on an ancient boat.
cur non singularis eius existimetur prudentia: See on 10.5 *nullam seiunctam sibi ab eo ... fortunam* for the effect of *eius*. The emphatic word here, *singularis*, functions as a predicate adjective modifying *prudentia*. The subjunctive is deliberative.

11.1 nihil aliud egit quam: "he did nothing but" + substantive clause of result.
<quam> plurimis ... auxilio: datives of reference and purpose. *quam plurimis* is an abbreviated form of the expression *tam plurimis quam posset*. See on 9.3 *quantum potuit ... texit* for another abbreviated correlative expression.
quibus rebus: ablative of means. For the form of the relative clause, see on 9.3 *quibus rebus indiguerunt, adiuuit*.
cui ... defuerit: "who lacked anything," literally "to whom anything was wanting." In other words, Atticus supplied all who came to him in Epirus with everything they needed. Nepos' fondness for negative turns of phrase gets in the way at times.
nemini non ... potestas facta est: another double negative for emphasis, "everyone was given the opportunity."
11.2 proelium Philippense: "the battle at Philippi"; there were actually two battles, 20 days apart, in October 42. The Caesarians Antony and Octavian combined their forces to defeat the Republicans led by M. Brutus and C. Cassius.
L. Iulium Mocillam: Not mentioned elsewhere, which is surprising considering his rank. The name may be corrupt in the manuscripts.
praetorium: "ex-praetor."
Aulumque Torquatum: A distant kinsman of Atticus' school-friend L. Torquatus (see on 1.4 *L. Torquatus*), he seems to have been quaestor in 43 under the consul Pansa and to have perished not long after Philippi.
perculsos < *percello*, "strike, dash down."
Samothraciam: It is not clear why the Republicans took refuge on this northeastern Aegean island.
supportari < *supporto*, "convey."
11.4 quod ... uenditauit: substantive *quod*-clause, which fills in the meaning of *id ... iudicari potest*. *uendito* is a frequentative verb derived from *uendo*, "give for sale."
qui ... coluerit: causal relative clause. *coluerit* < *colo*, "cultivate, devote one's self to."
11.5 neque ... non malebat obliuisci quam ulcisci: "wished rather to forget than to avenge"; yet another double negative.
quoad: "as long as."
11.6 sui cuique mores ... hominibus: "a man's character fashions his fate," more literally "for each man his own character fashions his fate." *hominibus* is plural because the phrase *sui cuique mores fingunt* is a generalization applicable to "all humans." This is a verse quotation (an iambic senarius) from an unknown play.
ne qua in re: "that in nothing."
iure: "with justice"; ablative of manner.
plecteretur < *plecto*, "punish."
12.1 M. Vipsanius Agrippa: Octavian's most successful general and most helpful friend. Like Octavian he made an accelerated progress up the

cursus honorum; he was consul at the age of 27 in 37 BC. It was at about this time that he married Atticus' daughter (born in 51).
adulescenti Caesari: the young Octavian, future emperor Augustus. He took the name C. Julius Caesar Octavianus when "adopted" by his great-uncle Julius Caesar in his will.
cum ... haberet: concessive.
nullius condicionis non ... potestatem: "the power to make any terms [he liked]"; another double negative.
potissimum: "in preference to all others."
eius: Atticus'.
praeoptaret equitis Romani filiam generosarum nuptiis: "he liked the daughter of a Roman *eques* better than marriage with [one of the] well-born ladies."

12.2 **harum nuptiarum conciliator:** Antony must have wanted to fortify his uneasy alliance with Octavian by joining Atticus, who had proven his loyalty to Antony, to Agrippa, a steadfast partisan of Octavian. Antony himself had already married Octavian's sister Octavia, but further links would not have come amiss.
triumuir rei publicae: The full name of the office was *triumuir rei publicae constituendae* "member of a board of three appointed for the [re-]establishing of the constitution." Antony, Octavian and Lepidus were "appointed" to this board by the Senate in November of 43 for an initial term of 5 years.
cuius: Antony's.
cum ... posset: concessive. The subject is Atticus.
ea: The antecedent is *gratia*.
in deprecandis ... periculis: gerund-replacing gerundive, standing in for *in pericula deprecando*. See on 2.5 *multiplicandis usuris*. *deprecandis* < *deprecor*, "ward off, avert."

12.3 **L. Saufei equitis Romani:** His philosophical leanings (like those of Atticus) were towards Epicurean doctrine. Cicero didn't think much of his friend's friend.
fieret certior < *certior fio*, "I am informed."
recuperasse = *recuperauisse*, "recovered."

12.4 **idem L. Iulium Calidum ... expediuit:** A long and wandering sentence, but typical in its structure : (1) subject (*idem* = Atticus), (2) object (*Calidum* and all its modifiers, *uirum bonum, eruditum, absentem* and *relatum*), (3) verb (*expediuit*).
L. Iulium Calidum: Calidus, despite his excellent qualifications, is not mentioned elsewhere. This leads many to believe that the name has been garbled in transmission. Catullus' friend L. Licinius Calvus is a popular substitute.
quem ... tulisse aetatem: *aetatem* is the accusative subject of the indirect statement depending on *contendere*; *quem* is the direct object of *tulisse*.
uideor posse contendere: "it seems to me that I can say," literally "I seem to be able to assert." Nepos is not very assertive with his claim.

in proscriptorum numero ... absentem relatum: predicate modifiers of *Calidum*; "when [Calidus] although absent, had been entered into the number of the proscribed."
a P. Volumnio: See on 9.4 *P. uero Volumnio*. Volumnius owed Atticus a large debt of gratitude.
praefecto fabrum: One assumes that originally the *praefectus fabrum* ("chief of the builders") was responsible for the "engineers" of the Roman army, but in this period the title was used for the confidential aide to the commander.

12.5 **quod ... utrum ... fuerit:** "and whether this was"; indirect question after *iudicare*.
non secus ... quam: "not otherwise ... than, the same ... as."
Attico ... curae : dative of reference and dative of purpose.

13.1 **cum esset:** concessive.
emax: "fond of buying"; the adjective is derived from *emo*, "buy."

13.2 **colle Quirinali:** the most northerly of the seven hills of Rome.
Tamphilianam: a house named after the man who had it built, or a former owner, one Tamphilius.
antiquitus: "long ago"; an adverb.
plus salis quam sumptus habebat: "was tasteful rather than expensive," literally "had more of good taste than of expense." *salis* and *sumptus* are partitive genitives.

13.3 **familia:** the domestic (slave) staff.
anagnostae: "readers," nominative plural masculine; a Greek word.
ne pedisequus quidem: "not even a page-boy."
utrumque horum: "both of these"; i.e., both reading aloud and copying.
cultus domesticus: i.e., "the running of a civilized house."
adprime: "exceedingly"; an adverb more colloquial than literary.

13.4 **factum:** "trained."
non intemperanter concupiscere ... debet duci: "not having uncontrolled desires ought to be considered."
quod ... uideas: The antecedent of *quod* is *intemperanter concupiscere*. The subjunctive is potential.
continentis: "[characteristic] of a self-restrained man."
parare ... non mediocris est industriae: "obtaining ... is [characteristic] of remarkable industry."

13.5 **supellex:** "furnishings."
ut in neutram partem conspici posset: "so that it was conspicuous in neither direction"; i.e., neither extravagant nor mean.

13.6 **leue:** The "antecedent" of *leue* ought to be the direct object of *praeteribo*, but Nepos gets a bit lost in his subordinate clauses, and has to start afresh with *scimus*. This type of construction is called anacoluthon, meaning "it does not follow."
uisum iri: "that it will seem," literally "that there is a going [*iri*] to seem [*uisum*, supine]." This construction is used in indirect statement

when a future passive infinitive (which Latin doesn't have) is needed. See AG 509.
cum ... esset: concessive.
non parum liberaliter: "with abundant generosity."
amplius: comparative adjective modifying *expensum*.
terna milia peraeque in singulos menses: *terna* and *singulos* are distributive numerals, *peraeque* ("equally") stresses the evenness of the distributions; Atticus spent no more than three thousand sesterces *per month* on entertainment.
ephemeride < *ephemeris*, "account book."
expensum ... ferre: "enter as [a sum] paid out." *expensum* < *expendo*, "weigh out, pay." The use of *fero* to mean "enter" is a bit of technical accounting vocabulary.

14.1 **acroama:** "performance," nominative singular neuter; a Greek word.
anagnosten: "reader"; the word has a Greek accusative singular masculine ending.
neque umquam ... cenatum est: "nor was there ever a dinner"; impersonal passive.
conuiuae: "fellow-diners," nominative plural masculine (declines like *poeta*).

14.2 **uocabat:** "invited."
tanta ... accessio: i.e., the inheritance from his uncle.
sestertio uicies: *uicies* is a "multiplier," as is the *centena milia* customarily omitted in sums of money (see on 5.2 *centies sestertium*). So the sum that Atticus inherited from his father was 20 times 100 times a thousand, or 2 million sesterces, 1/5 the size of his uncle's estate.
parique fastigio steterit: "and he stood on a like eminence."

14.3 **Arretinum et Nomentanum:** Near modern Arezzo and Mentana.
usum < *usus, -us*, "usefulness, value."
non magnitudine, sed ratione: "not by the total, but by the account book." In other words, he preferred income-producing properties to luxury estates.
metiri < *metior*, "measure out."

15.1 **comitas:** "affability, companionable nature."
difficile ... intellectu: "difficult to understand"; a small number of adjectives (*difficile, incredibile, mirabile, horribile*, etc.) are used with the supine in *-u*, which denotes the action which the adjective describes. See AG 510.
religiose: "scrupulously."
liberalis: genitive, as is *leuis* (see below).
leuis arbitrabatur polliceri: "he thought it [characteristic] of a fickle man to promise."

15.2 **in tuendo:** "in watching over [something]." The object is the implied antecedent of *quod. tuendo* < *tueor*.
quod semel annuisset: "if once he had promised it"; conditional relative clause. *annuisset* < *annuo*, "nod assent."
mandatam: sc. *rem*, "a commission."

pertaesum est < *pertaedet*, "it is exceedingly vexatious." This impersonal expression takes the genitive of the vexatious object and accusative of the person vexed. In the perfect tenses the verb is deponent. English idiom requires translating the verb personally and treating the genitive as its subject: "business never vexed him."
agi: "was involved."
qua: ablative of comparison after *carius*; the antecedent is *existimationem*.

15.3 M. Catonis: The famous Cato, who took his life at Utica to avoid being offered a pardon by Caesar. Atticus' oversight of his affairs is not elsewhere attested.
iudicari poterat ... fugisse: "one can judge that he avoided," literally "he was able to be judged to have avoided." This expression differs from that in 5.3 (*ut iudicari possit ... ualere similitudinem*) in that the construction here is personal (i.e., has a person [Atticus] as subject of *poterat*), while that at 5.3 is impersonal (the accusative/infinitive clause functions as the "subject" of *possit*).
rei publicae procurationem: Atticus never held or (apparently) aspired to public office.

16.1 quam quod adulescens idem ... fuit: "than that the same man was as a young man."
cum aequalibus uixit: *uixit* is a second verb for the *quod*-clause, i.e., it constitutes more of the "evidence" for Atticus' humane character. *uiuere cum aliquo* means "to spend a lot of time with someone."

16.2 quamquam: "and yet"; connects its clause with what went before.
ei: Cicero.

16.3 ei rei ... indicio: datives of reference and purpose.
eos libros: Atticus is the dedicatee of Cicero's treatises *de Amicitia* and *de Senectute*, and a speaker in the dialogues *de Legibus, Brutus, Academica Posteriora*, and *de Finibus*.
in uulgus ... editi: "published." *editi* < *edo*, "give out."
undecim uolumina epistularum ... missarum: Modern editions have 16 volumes of letters to Atticus. The collection begins shortly before Cicero's consulship and stops a full year before Cicero's assassination (contradicting Nepos' phrase *ad extremum tempus*). This remains a mystery.
quae qui legat: "and if one reads these"; conditional relative clause. *quae* is a connecting relative.
multum: internal or adverbial accusative. See AG 390c.
contextam < *contexo*, "weave together."

16.4 ut ... appareat: See on 5.3 *ut ... possit* for the primary tense *appareat* after the perfect tense verb *perscripta sunt*.
prudentiam ... esse diuinationem: "that his guessing was ... foresight." *prudentia* < *pro-uidentia*; it is a predicate noun here. The accusative/infinitive phrase functions as the "subject" of the impersonal expression *existimari possit*.
quodam modo: "somehow," literally "in a certain way."

quae nunc usu ueniunt: "which are coming [to pass] in the course of events." The precise reference of *nunc* is not easy to determine. Chapters 1-18 of the *Life* appear to have been written before Atticus' death in 32 (and the historical situation referred to in 12.1 could not have been described before 36/35); chapters 19-22 are an appendix added between 32 and 27 (Octavian is never called Augustus).
cecinit < *cano*, "sing, speak impressively or solemnly."

17.1 **quid plura commemorem:** "why should I make more remarks?"; deliberative subjunctive.
cum hoc ipsum ... gloriantem audierim: "because I heard Atticus himself expressing his pride in the fact that." Verbs of sense perception like *audio* sometimes govern an accusative + participle clause (*ipsum gloriantem*). Contrast the accusative + infinitive clause *dolores ... accessisse sensit* in 21.4. *hoc* is the object of *gloriantem*, and is further defined by the indirect statement *se ... redisse* below.
extulit < *effero*, "carry out for burial, bear to the grave."
annorum nonaginta: "when she was 90"; *annorum* is a partitive genitive.
<complesset> = *compleuisset*. The subject is Atticus.
se numquam cum matre in gratiam redisse: "that he had never gotten back into his mother's good graces"; i.e., his mother had never been angry at him (see 17.2).
simultate < *simultas*, "quarrel."

17.2 **inter eos:** Atticus and his mother, and Atticus and his sister, respectively.
querimoniam: "grounds for complaint."
ea ... indulgentia: ablative of description.
in suos: Nepos is generalizing from Atticus' relations with his mother and sister to his overall *pietas* (*in suos*).
irasci eis nefas duceret: "he believed it wrong to be angry with those." *irascor*, "be angry" + dative.

17.3 **natura:** ablative of cause.
paremus < *pareo*, "obey" + dative.
ita percepta habuit praecepta: *percepta* < *percipio*, "understand thoroughly." Nepos is indulging in a little word-play. *habuit* is very like an auxiliary verb here; see AG 497b.
ad uitam agendam: See on 9.3 *ad Antonium violandum*.

18.1 **ordinauit:** "set in order." Atticus' one-volume *liber annalis* ("book of years"), written between 50 and 47, gave a year-by-year list of Roman consuls over a period of 700+ years (insofar as they could be determined) together with a thumbnail sketch of each year's events. It was used by Cicero, Nepos and Velleius Paterculus (at the very least), but only a few scraps survive.

18.2 **subtexuit** < *subtexo*, "weave onto, subjoin."
propagines: "progeny, descendants."

18.3 **Iuniam familiam:** Brutus' family name, his *nomen*, was Junius.

qui a quoque ortus: relative clause, modifying the subject of *cepisset*. *ortus* < *orior*, "come forth, originate."

quos honores quibusque temporibus cepisset: indirect questions dependent on *notans*. *honores* < *honos* or *honor*, "elective office." Atticus' work, which sounds like a glorified family tree, treated the progeny of great men as well as the great men themselves.

18.4 **Marcelli Claudi:** sc. *rogatu*. There were several prominent men of this name active in the last decades of the Republic. This is probably C. Claudius Marcellus, cos. 50, who died in 40 BC. His wife was Octavian's sister Octavia, his son the Marcellus who was heir apparent when he died in 23 BC at the age of 19. Each of the three men referred to here (Claudius Marcellus, Cornelius Scipio, Fabius Maximus) bears the name of one of Rome's most cherished heroes. M. Claudius Marcellus was the conqueror of Rome's first overseas province, Sicily. Q. Fabius Maximus Cunctator was the man who wore down Hannibal by delaying (in the Second Punic War). P. Cornelius Scipio Africanus and his grandson by adoption Aemilianus likewise distinguished themselves against Carthaginian foes, among others. Aemilianus was the son of L. Aemilius Paullus, conqueror of the last king of Macedon.

Marcellorum: Nepos expresses himself very concisely here. The full form of the thought is *familiam Marcellorum a stirpe ad hanc aetatem ordine enumerauit*.

Scipionis Cornelii: sc. *rogatu*. The identity of this man is not certain.

Fabii Maximi: sc. *rogatu*. Consul of 45 BC.

Fabiorum et Aemiliorum: See above on *Marcellorum*.

quibus libris: ablative of comparison after *dulcius*.

iis: dative of reference; antecedent of *qui*.

notitiae < *notitia*, "knowledge."

clarorum uirorum: objective genitive.

18.5 **<artem> ... poeticen:** "the art of poetry." Nepos uses an accusative singular feminine Greek ending (*-en*) for the Greek adjective.

18.6 **exposuit** < *expono*, "set out, exhibit"; the object is the unexpressed antecedent of the relative clause *qui ... praestiterunt*.

quaternis quinisue uersibus: "by verses, no more than four or five each." *quaternis* and *quinis* are distributive numerals. None of Atticus' verses survive.

quod: "and as for this"; connecting relative.

credendum sit: potential subjunctive. The accusative/infinitive clause *tantas res ... potuisse declarari* ("that such great matters were able to be expressed") functions as the subject of *sit*.

unus liber Graece confectus: This is not extant.

19.1 **Hactenus:** "up to this point." *tenus* is a post-positive preposition meaning "as far as."

edita < *edo*, "publish." *edita* is neuter plural, nominative, and refers to the first 18 chapters of the *Life*.

superstites ei esse: "to have outlived him [Atticus]." *superstites* < *superstes*, "survivor"; plural, to agree with *nos*.
quantum potuerimus: "insofar as I am able," literally "as much as I will have been able." English usage is comfortable with a present tense here, but Latin requires a future perfect.
lectores docebimus ... mores ... conciliare: *docebimus* has two objects, the first *lectores*, the second the accusative/infinitive clause *mores ... conciliare*.
suos cuique mores: "the character of each man," literally "for each man, his character"; an indirect (and slightly modified) statement of the maxim quoted at 11.6 above.
plerumque: "generally."
19.2 **imperatoris Diui filii:** "of the emperor, the son of the Divine [Julius]." The reference to Caesar's deification (42 BC) began appearing in Octavian's titulature in 40 BC.
ante: "before this"; an adverb.
ceperat: "he had won over."
principes ciuitatis dignitate pari: *dignitate pari* is an ablative of description. Nepos uses *princeps* as it was used throughout the Republic, to indicate any outstanding figure in the state.
19.3 **Caesarem:** Octavian, not Julius.
quod ... detulerit: relative clause of characteristic modifying *nihil*.
conciliarit = *conciliauerit*, "brought [to him]."
quod ... quiuit consequi: The antecedent of this clause is the direct object of *conciliarit*, but it has been omitted. See AG 307c. *quiuit* < *queo*, "be able."
19.4 **neptis:** "granddaughter." Her name was Vipsania Agrippina.
hanc: the granddaughter.
anniculam: "as a girl of nine years."
Ti. Claudio Neroni, Drusilla nato, priuigno suo: The future emperor Tiberius, elder son of Livia (here called Drusilla) by her first marriage, hence Octavian's step-son. At the time of his betrothal, he was not directly in line to succeed Octavian. When he became the heir apparent, he had to divorce Vipsania and marry Augustus' daughter Julia. *Drusilla* is an ablative of source.
despondit < *despondeo*, "betroth."
eorum: of Atticus and Octavian.
sanxit < *sancio*, "confirm, render inviolable."
20.1 **quamuis:** "and yet."
haec sponsalia: "this betrothal." *sponsalia* is a neuter plural adjective meaning originally "things pertaining to a betrothal," hence is used in the plural of a single betrothal.
non solum: looks forward to the *sed etiam* in 20.2.
abesset: The subject is Octavian.
quin Attico mitteret: "without sending [one] to Atticus"; negative adverbial result clause.

quid ageret ... quid legeret ... quibusque in locis et quamdiu esset moraturus: indirect questions reporting the usual contents of Octavian's letters to Atticus. *esset moraturus* (< *moror*, "tarry") is a periphrastic form used in secondary sequence indirect questions to replace a future indicative. See AG 575a.

20.2 in urbe: "in Rome."
frueretur < *fruor*, "enjoy [the company] of" + ablative.
temere: "by chance"; in other words, if ever Octavian failed to write to Atticus, there was a good reason for it.
modo ... modo ... interdum: "sometimes ... at other times ... occasionally."
eliceret < *elicio*, "call forth, elicit."

20.3 aedis Iouis Feretrii: The original temple of Jupiter Feretrius (< *ferio*, "strike" i.e., with a bolt of lightning) was said to be a foundation of Romulus himself (See Livy 1.10.6). The restoration referred to here contributed to the image of Augustus as Rome's second founder. Among the temple-building projects proudly listed by Augustus in his *Res Gestae* this appears first.
detecta < *detego*, "uncover"; nominative.
prolaberetur < *prolabor*, "slip down, go to ruin."
ut ... curaret: substantive result clause, functioning as the "subject" of the impersonal verb *accidit*. See AG 569.2.
eam reficiendam: gerund-replacing gerundive, standing in for *eam reficiendum*, where the gerund *reficiendum* is the object of *curaret*, and *eam* is the object of *reficiendum*. See on 2.5 *multiplicandis usuris*.

20.4 absens: "apart." Antony was fighting or administering provinces in the East for much of the period 42-32.
colebatur < *colo*, "cultivate, devote oneself to, treat with respect."
ut ... curae sibi haberet ... certiorem facere: "that he took care to inform." *curae* and *sibi* are datives of purpose and reference. *certiorem facere* ("to inform") is the active form of *certior fio* (see on 12.3 *fieret certior*). The infinitive *facere* functions as the "object" of *haberet*.
ex ultimis terris: In 36 Antony was involved in a (disastrous) expedition against the Parthian kingdom, which was situated (roughly) where modern Iran is.
quid ageret: indirect question specifying what information Antony communicated to Atticus.

20.5 hoc quale sit: "what kind of achievement this is"; indirect question dependent on *existimabit*. "This" refers to the activities reported in the preceding sentence.
quantae sit sapientiae: "how much skill it takes," literally "of how much skill it is characteristic." The meaning of "it" is defined by the infinitive + direct object phrase *retinere usum beneuolentiamque*.
eorum: goes with *usum beneuolentiamque* and refers to Octavian and Antony.
aemulatio: "rivalry."
obtrectatio: "conflict."

Suggestions for Further Reading

On Nepos as an author:
J. Geiger, *Cornelius Nepos and Ancient Political Biography*. *Hermes Einzelschriften* 47 (Stuttgart, 1985).
N. Horsfall, *Cornelius Nepos, a Selection, Including the Lives of Cato and Atticus* (Oxford, 1989). (This book contains a translation of the *Life* and a detailed historical commentary.)

On Nepos' text:
P. K. Marshall, *Cornelii Nepotis vitae cum fragmentis* (Leipzig, 1985).
P. K. Marshall, *The Manuscript Tradition of Cornelius Nepos*. University of London, Institute of Classical Studies, *Bulletin Supplement* no. 37 (London, 1977).

On the period:
The best things to read, as Nepos himself says, are Cicero's letters to Atticus.
D. R. Shackelton Bailey, *Cicero, Letters to Atticus*, 7 vols. (Cambridge, 1965-70) provides both translation and commentary. On Atticus, see especially vol. 1, pp. 3-59.

For the intellectual context:
E. Rawson, *The Intellectual Life of the Late Roman Republic* (London, 1985).